The Reproductive System

Injury, Illness and Health

Steve Parker

www.heinemann.co.uk/library
Visit our website to find out more information about **Heinemann Library** books.

To order:
☎ Phone 44 (0) 1865 888066
🖹 Send a fax to 44 (0) 1865 314091
💻 Visit the Heinemann Bookshop at www.heinemann.co.uk/library to browse our catalogue and order online.

First published in Great Britain by Heinemann Library, Halley Court, Jordan Hill, Oxford OX2 8EJ, part of Harcourt Education.

Heinemann is a registered trademark of Harcourt Education Ltd.

Editorial: Nick Hunter and Catherine Clarke
Design: Jo Hinton-Malivoire and
Tinstar Design Limited (www.tinstar.co.uk)
Illustrations: Ken Vail Graphic Design
Picture Research: Maria Joannou and
Su Alexander
Production: Viv Hichens

Originated by Ambassador Litho Ltd
Printed and bound in Hong Kong, China by
South China Printing Company

ISBN 0 431 15719 7
07 06 05 04 03
10 9 8 7 6 5 4 3 2 1

British Library Cataloguing in Publication Data
Parker, Steve
Reproductive System. – (Body Focus)
612.6
A full catalogue record for this book is available from the British Library.

Acknowledgements
The publishers would like to thank the following for permission to reproduce photographs:

Corbis pp. 5 (Jennie Woodcock), 30 (Jules Perrier), 31 (Jon Spaull), 42; Corbis Stock Market pp. 4 (Tom & Dee Ann McCarthy) 25 (Pete Saloutos), 33 (Ariel Skelley), 34 (Jon Feingersh), 35, 43 (George Shelley); Network p.30 (Barry Lewis); Science Photo Library pp. 7 (Simon Fraser), 10 (Professors P. M. Motta & J. Van Blerkom), 12 (Laurent, Yakou), 14 (Dr E. Walker), 15 (Keith, Custom Medical Stock Photo), 17, 19 (Professor S Cinti, CNRI), 20, 21 (Gary Carlson), 22 (CNRI), 26 (K. H. Kjeldsen), 27 (D. Phillips), 28 (Pascal Goetgheluck), 29 (Hank Morgan), 37 (Oscar Burriel), 39 (Adam Hart Davis), 41 (James King Holmes); Stone/Getty p. 40 (James Darell); Telegraph Colour Library p. 24 (David McGlynn).

Cover photograph of a coloured X-ray showing the human female torso, with an artwork representation of the reproductive organs, reproduced with permission of Science Photo Library.

The publishers would like to thank David Wright for his assistance with the preparation of this book.

Every effort has been made to contact copyright holders of any material reproduced in this book. Any omissions will be rectified in subsequent printings if notice is given to the publishers.

CONTENTS

Words appearing in the text in bold, **like this**, are explained in the Glossary.

Reproduction means making or producing more of the same kind. It is a feature of life itself. All living things reproduce to make more of their kind. The parts of the body involved in making new individuals are known as the reproductive system.

The basic process of reproduction in humans, and the body parts involved, are much the same as in other animals. In particular, they are very similar to those of other mammals – warm-blooded animals with fur or hair, that feed their newborn on milk. In almost all mammals, the baby develops inside the female's body, in a specialized part called the womb or **uterus**. The baby leaves the womb during a process known as birth. After birth, the baby is fed on milk made by the mother.

Female and male

There are two kinds or sexes of human beings – female and male. Each has a different role in reproduction. Indeed, the major differences between the female human body and the male human body are in the reproductive parts themselves. Other differences are influenced by the way the reproductive parts work, and the products they make, such as **hormones**.

Reproduction makes not only more human beings, but also parents and children and families.

The reproductive system is the only system in the body that changes considerably after birth. During childhood its parts are present, but not fully developed or able to function. They develop to their mature, working condition usually during the early teenage years (although there is great individual variation). The process of change in the structure and function of the reproductive system, and the time when it occurs, are known as **puberty**.

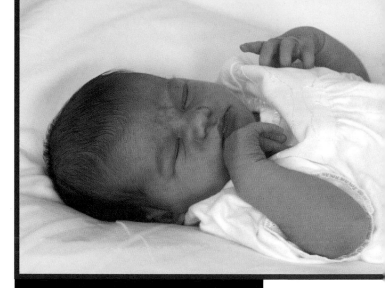

The day of birth may seem like 'day one', but life began nine months earlier.

The developing baby

All parts of the human body consist of microscopic **cells**. The female reproductive parts make special cells called **egg** cells. The male reproductive parts make microscopic cells called **sperm** cells. For reproduction, a sperm cell is transferred to the female body (during **sexual intercourse**) and joins with an egg cell. This joining is known as **fertilization**. The result is a fertilized egg called a zygote, which is even smaller than the head of a pin.

The fertilized egg grows and develops for nine months inside the uterus of the female. This time is known as pregnancy or **gestation**. During the earliest stages of development, until about eight weeks after fertilization, the new individual is known medically as an **embryo**. From about eight weeks after fertilization until birth, it is known as a **fetus** (foetus), and during this time the new life is recognizably human. In everyday terms, however, the developing individual before birth, and afterwards, is usually called the baby.

Views and attitudes

Sexual reproduction and the growth of a baby in the womb are entirely natural processes. However attitudes towards them vary hugely around the world – for example, how and when sex might occur, and whether a woman and man who produce a child should be in some form of partnership, such as marriage.

These views and attitudes vary between people of different cultures, traditions, ethnic groups, social backgrounds and faiths. Even though reproduction is a basic biological process, some people feel awkward or embarrassed when discussing sexual matters or problems of the reproductive system.

FEMALE REPRODUCTIVE ORGANS

The main parts of the female reproductive system are in the lower **abdomen** of the body. They consist of the **ovaries**, the **uterine tubes** (also called fallopian tubes or oviducts), the **uterus** (womb) and the **vagina**.

Ovaries

The two ovaries are the main female reproductive parts or organs, and they are positioned one in either side of the lower abdomen. They produce the **egg** cells, and retain them until each one ripens and is released. The ovaries also make natural body chemicals called **hormones**, that control the female cycle of fertility – the times when it is possible to begin or **conceive** a baby, and when it is not.

Each ovary is about half the size of a hen's egg. The inner structure of the ovary, and how the egg cells develop inside it, are shown on the following pages.

Medicine and reproduction

The workings of the reproductive system can be altered by many kinds of medical procedures and modern technologies. This applies to both the female and male systems. Often the aim is not so much to treat a health problem in the individual concerned. The aim is to make it possible for an individual person to become a parent – or to do the opposite, and prevent conception of a baby after sex (known as contraception).

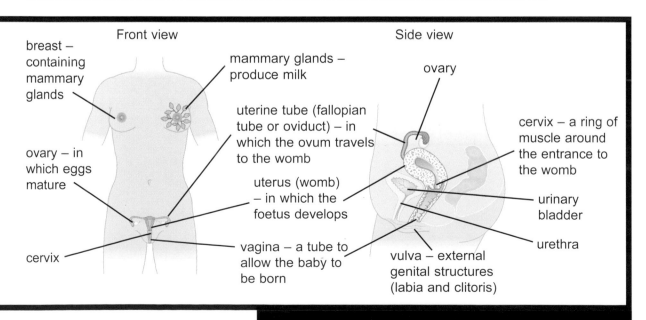

Front view

breast – containing mammary glands

mammary glands – produce milk

ovary – in which eggs mature

uterine tube (fallopian tube or oviduct) – in which the ovum travels to the womb

uterus (womb) – in which the foetus develops

cervix

vagina – a tube to allow the baby to be born

Side view

ovary

cervix – a ring of muscle around the entrance to the womb

urinary bladder

urethra

vulva – external genital structures (labia and clitoris)

This diagram shows the female reproductive organs.

Uterine tubes

Each of the two uterine tubes links an ovary with the uterus (womb). The tube is about 10 centimetres long, and it carries a ripened egg from the ovary to the uterus. At the ovary end, it widens out into a funnel shape that has a wavy or finger-like edge. This wraps around part of the ovary, like a grasping hand. At the other end of the uterine tube, the tunnel within it opens into the space inside the uterus.

Uterus (womb)

The uterus is a pear-shaped organ in the base of the lower abdomen. Its thinner end points down and back, and its thicker end tilts up and forwards, above the **bladder**. The uterus is, in effect, a container with very thick, muscular walls. The space inside the uterus is usually very small and squashed almost flat, except

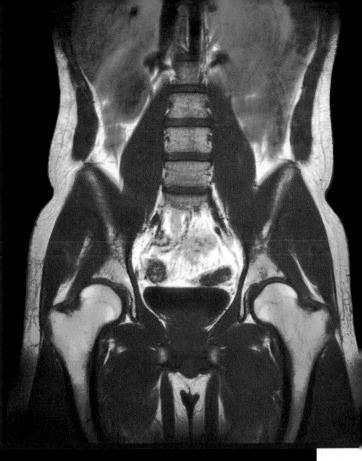

An ultrasound scan of female reproductive parts (see diagram opposite).

during pregnancy when the uterus enlarges greatly as the baby develops inside it. In a woman who has not had children, the whole uterus is slightly smaller than her clenched fist. After bearing children it is usually larger.

Vagina

The lower, narrower end of the uterus is called the neck or **cervix**. It opens into the vagina, also known as the birth canal. This is a flexible tube that opens to the external genital parts, the vulva, between the legs. During birth, the baby leaves the uterus and passes through the vagina to reach the outside world.

Mammary glands

A newborn human baby usually feeds on milk made by the mother's two **mammary glands**. These are within the breasts on the chest. The milk they produce has precisely the right amounts of **nutrients** including sugars, fats, **proteins**, vitamins and minerals, for the new baby. The mammary glands are generally regarded as part of the female reproductive system. However babies can thrive on non-human milk, including special formula milks prepared from powders or concentrates.

A woman cannot **conceive** a baby at any time. The female reproductive system works in a rhythmical fashion called the fertility cycle or **menstrual cycle**. A typical cycle lasts for about 28 days and then begins again. It is only possible to conceive a baby during a few days within each cycle.

Ripening of the egg

During the first part of each cycle, an **egg** cell in one of the **ovaries** becomes mature or ripe. The egg develops within its tiny container, or capsule known as the **follicle**. In a typical menstrual cycle, the ripening of the egg begins at days 1–2, and continues for the next 12–13 days.

Release of the egg

On day 14 of the typical cycle, the ripe egg is released from its follicle – a process known as **ovulation**. The ripe egg passes into the funnel-shaped end of the **uterine tube**, and moves along the tube to the **uterus**. If **fertilization** of the egg by a **sperm** is to occur, it is most likely during the egg's journey along the uterine tube.

In the meantime, from about days 5–6 of the cycle, the inner lining of the uterus starts to become thick with **nutrients** and blood-rich tissues. This makes the lining, which is known as the **endometrium**, able to receive and nourish a fertilized egg, so that it can begin to develop into a baby.

Control of the menstrual cycle

Natural body chemicals called **hormones** control the female menstrual cycle. There are four main hormones involved:
- FSH, follicle-stimulating hormone, is released by the pituitary gland just below the brain. It stimulates an egg to ripen, in the first part of the cycle.
- **oestrogen** (estrogen) is produced by the ripening follicle, and causes thickening of the uterus lining
- LH, luteinizing hormone, is also released by the pituitary. It causes the follicle to release its egg and then change into another structure, the corpus luteum.
- progesterone is produced by the corpus luteum, which also makes some oestrogen. These two hormones maintain the thickened uterus lining until the cycle ends.

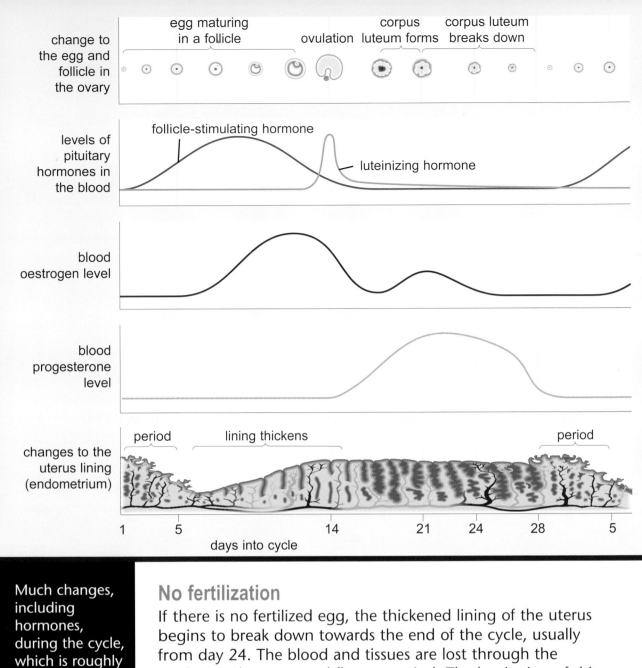

change to the egg and follicle in the ovary — egg maturing in a follicle / ovulation / corpus luteum forms / corpus luteum breaks down

levels of pituitary hormones in the blood — follicle-stimulating hormone / luteinizing hormone

blood oestrogen level

blood progesterone level

changes to the uterus lining (endometrium) — period / lining thickens / period

days into cycle — 1 5 14 21 24 28 5

Much changes, including hormones, during the cycle, which is roughly 28 days.

No fertilization

If there is no fertilized egg, the thickened lining of the uterus begins to break down towards the end of the cycle, usually from day 24. The blood and tissues are lost through the **vagina** as the menstrual flow or period. The beginning of this loss marks the end of one cycle, at day 28 and the start of a new cycle, at day 1 again. The period usually lasts 3–5 days.

PMS or PMT

Premenstrual syndrome, PMS, usually occurs in the few days before a period starts. There are often alterations in mood, feelings and emotions, along with changes in the physical body, such as enlarged and tender breasts, a bloated feeling in the stomach and swollen ankles. An alternative name is PMT, premenstrual tension, due to feelings of being nervous and 'on edge'.

A typical ripe **egg** cell, also called an **ovum**, is about 0.1 millimetres across. Compared to other cells in the body, this is relatively huge. It is far larger than the equivalent male cell, the **sperm**.

Formation of egg cells

When a baby girl is born, there are around 300,000 unripe egg cells in each **ovary**. Many of these gradually break up, or disintegrate during childhood. By the time of **puberty**, there are around 150,000. On average, during the years when a woman is able to have children (approximately between 15 and 50 years of age), about 400–500 eggs will ripen and be released. Usually one egg is released in each **menstrual cycle**, from alternate ovaries.

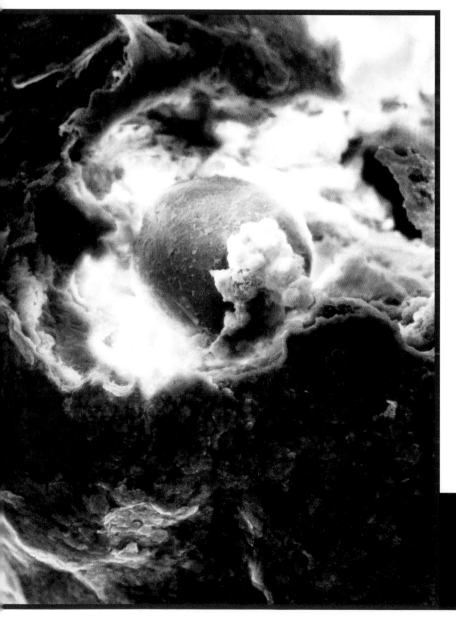

The ripening follicle

At the start of the menstrual cycle, during days 1–5, several egg cells are stimulated to ripen and their **follicles** enlarge. By day 6, one of these has become 'dominant' and continues its development, while the others shrink away. The dominant follicle becomes larger, and the cells forming its outer layers produce the **hormone oestrogen**. A **nutrient**-rich fluid collects inside the follicle, nourishing the egg cell as it passes through its final stages of ripening.

A ripe egg cell is released, or ovulated, from its follicle (container). It floats into the fluid inside the uterine tube.

Ovulation

The fully ripe follicle, called a graafian follicle, is about 2 millimetres across. On or around day 14 of the cycle, the follicle 'explodes' and propels the ripe, mature egg cell into the nearby funnel-shaped end of the **uterine tube**. It is now ready to be **fertilized** by a sperm cell. The 'explosive' release of the egg cell from the follicle is called **ovulation**.

Multiple births

In most cases, only one baby at a time develops in the **uterus**. In other cases there are multiple pregnancies – twins, triplets and so on.

For non-identical twins, two eggs are released from the ovary at about the same time. Each egg is fertilized by a sperm, and develops from the start as a separate individual. The twins are as similar as ordinary brothers or sisters but not identical. For identical twins, the two individuals come from the same fertilized egg, so they have exactly the same **genes**. Identical twins are always the same sex – either both girls or both boys – and they look very similar.

Cell division – mitosis and meiosis

Each cell in the human body contains **genetic** material, in the form of the substance **DNA**. (Genes are the instructions for how the body develops, grows and carries out life processes.) Each body cell has two complete sets of genetic material. One came originally from the mother, and one from the father. The genetic material is packaged into tiny, thread-like structures called **chromosomes** inside the cell. There are two sets of 23 chromosomes, 46 in total, and this double-set is known as diploid.

New body cells are formed by division, or splitting of other cells. Cell division occurs to add extra cells during growth, to repair injured parts, and to replace old, worn-out cells as part of regular body maintenance. Ordinary body cells divide by a process called **mitosis**. During it, both sets of genetic material are copied.

Egg and sperm cells are produced by a different type of cell division, called **meiosis**. The original cell divides to form four resulting cells, not two. Also, the genetic material is halved to one set, of 23 chromosomes, in each egg or sperm. This is known as haploid or monoploid. Then, when egg and sperm join, the double-set will be restored.

The timing of the female or **menstrual cycle**, and length of its different stages, may vary greatly both between individual women, and in the same woman over time or with changing circumstances. Most women come to know their own cycle, and how their bodies work and feel. Changes should be reported to a doctor, although usually there is no cause for concern.

Menstrual problems

Most problems with the menstrual cycle are due to changes caused by the **hormones** that control and coordinate the cycle.

Dysmenorrhoea involves discomfort or pain in the lower **abdomen**, at or around the time of the period. It is often called 'period pain', and it may be due to spasm or contraction of the muscles in the **uterus** wall.

Menorrhagia is a heavier than normal menstrual flow or bleeding. It may or may not be accompanied by pain. Amenorrhoea is when menstrual cycles and their periods cease altogether. It can be caused by ill health, or loss of weight due to another health problem. Oligomenorrhoea is infrequent or longer than usual cycles, which again, may be due to another illness.

Around the time of their periods, women often experience pain or discomfort in the lower abdomen.

Menopause

Menstrual cycles are likely to be quite changeable and erratic when they first begin, during **puberty**. Likewise, cycles become more variable in the year or two before the **menopause**, which is the time when they cease, usually around the ages of 50–54 years. The changes in the regular cycle and its hormones during the menopause can affect other parts of the body. There may be hot flushes or sweats, heart palpitations, joint pains, mood swings, headaches and weak bones.

Effects of the menopause

The female hormones that control the menstrual cycle can also affect other body systems and functions. One effect of the menopause, in about one woman in five, is considerable weakening of the bones, which become brittle and fragile. This is known as osteoporosis. It may cause backache, and the bones are more likely to break during a fall or similar accident.

A healthy diet and plenty of exercise during earlier years encourages strong bones, which can better withstand menopausal changes. Treatment with hormone-containing tablets, known as hormone replacement therapy (HRT), also helps to protect against osteoporosis and ease other symptoms of the menopause.

Endometriosis

Sometimes small pieces or fragments of the uterus lining (**endometrium**) find their way, not out of the body as usual, but along a uterine tube and into the lower body cavity. Each month the pieces become rich with blood, and then break down, as they would do in their normal site. This is known as endometriosis. However the blood cannot escape, and it may irritate the parts around such as the intestines or **ovaries**. Symptoms include dragging pains and extra amounts of normal period bleeding. Treatment may include hormone tablets, and perhaps surgery to remove the fragments.

Treatments

There are various underlying causes of menstrual problems. Some are described on the following pages. In other cases they are due to an imbalance of the hormones that control the cycle, or there may be no obvious physical cause.

Modern medical treatments, such as pills or tablets that affect the hormonal cycle, are usually successful in reducing pain and other menstrual symptoms. The contraceptive pill can be especially useful for this.

Various combinations of surgery and/or medical drugs are usually successful for treating the conditions described below. Unlike body parts such as the heart or brain, most of the reproductive organs do not carry out vital life processes, so they are not essential for basic survival. However, general health measures and regular check-ups are vital.

Ovarian problems

An ovarian cyst is a fluid-filled bag in the **ovary**. It may be small and painless or it may grow larger, and interfere with **hormone** production and the **menstrual cycle**. It can cause pain, and press on the nearby **bladder**. The causes of ovarian cysts are unclear, although some result from abnormal ripening of an **egg** in its **follicle**.

Very rarely, an ovarian cyst may become malignant or cancerous. Again, the reasons for this change are not usually clear. The malignancy tends to cause vague symptoms in the early stages, such as discomfort in the lower **abdomen**. Later symptoms include weight loss and abdominal pain. Treatment may be a combination of surgery, radiotherapy (radiation treatment) and anti-cancer drugs.

Cervical problems

In cervical dysplasia, the cells that form the **cervix** lining change, and there is an increased risk of further cancerous changes in the future.

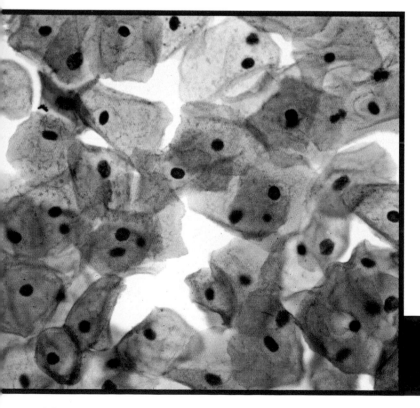

What triggers these alterations is not clear, but cervical cancer is one of the most common cancers affecting women. It causes abnormal vaginal discharge and bleeding, pain and general ill health. Treatment may be a combination of surgery, radiotherapy and anti-cancer drugs. The surgery usually includes removal of the **uterus**, known as a hysterectomy, and perhaps the ovaries and other reproductive parts.

Cervical cells taken during a 'smear' test are studied under a microscope. These cells are healthy.

A less serious cause of similar symptoms to cancer of the cervix, is cervical polyp, a bulging, grape-like growth of the lining. This can usually be removed during an operation.

Uterus problems

Fibroids are benign (non-cancerous) growths in the muscular wall of the uterus, or on its surface. In many cases they appear for no clear reason. Symptoms include heavy and painful periods, and perhaps a hard lump in the lower abdomen. Small fibroids that do not cause problems may simply be monitored at check-ups, but larger or troublesome ones are surgically removed.

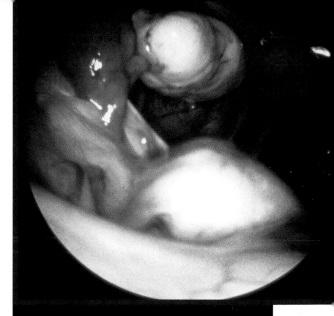

A narrow 'telescope' called a laparoscope allows doctors to examine reproductive and other parts inside the abdomen. This view is of healthy ovaries, fallopian tube and uterus.

Cancer of the uterus usually starts on the inside, in the lining or **endometrium**. It may cause vaginal discharge, painful periods, and irregular bleeding or 'spotting' between periods.

In a uterine prolapse, the muscles and **ligaments** that normally hold the uterus in place become loose and slack. This may happen after childbirth or with age. The uterus tends to sag and bulge downward into the **vagina**.

Other conditions

In some cases the reproductive system develops abnormally. A retroverted uterus slopes up and rearwards, rather than up and forwards. In persistent cloaca, the opening from the reproductive system (vagina) is shared with those from the urinary and digestive tracts. The symptoms of such conditions vary enormously. In some cases they may cause inability to have children. Surgery can often correct the defect.

Cervical smear (pap) test

A common procedure at a health check or 'well-woman' clinic is the cervical smear or 'pap' test (the Papanicolaou stain test, named after the person who devised it). During a physical examination of the reproductive system, a small sample or 'smear' of microscopic cells and fluid is taken from the cervix, for later laboratory examination. The test detects abnormal changes, which could signify early stages of cervical dysplasia or cancer.

In the male human body, the main parts of the reproductive system are in the lower **abdomen** and just below it. They consist of the **testes**, **scrotum**, **epididymes**, **vas deferens** (ductus deferens), prostate gland, **seminal vesicles** and penis.

Testes and scrotum

The two testes (testicles) are contained in a bag of skin, the scrotum, below the lower front of the abdomen. The testes make the male reproductive cells – **sperm** cells. They also produce male sex **hormones**, the chief one being **testosterone**. This controls the production of sperm and also development of male bodily features such as facial hair, muscle bulk and a deep voice.

Each testis is about three-quarters the size of a hen's egg. Its inner structures, and how the sperm cells develop inside it, are shown on the following pages.

Epididymes

Each of the two testes is connected to an epididymis, a tube about six metres long. This is folded and coiled so greatly that it forms a mass only four centimetres long, draped over the top and side of the testis. The epididymis stores sperm cells after they have been produced in the testis, before they leave along the next part of the system, the vas (ductus) deferens.

Vas (ductus) deferens

Each vas deferens (ductus deferens or sperm duct) is a tube-shaped continuation of the epididymis, about 20 centimetres long. It curves

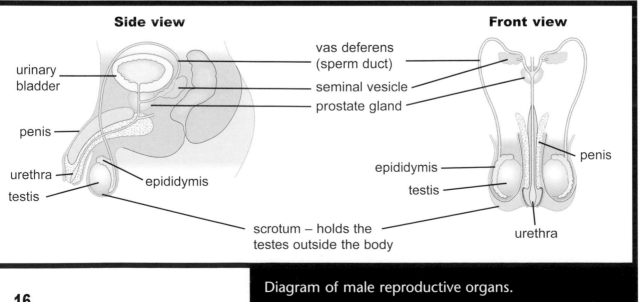

Diagram of male reproductive organs.

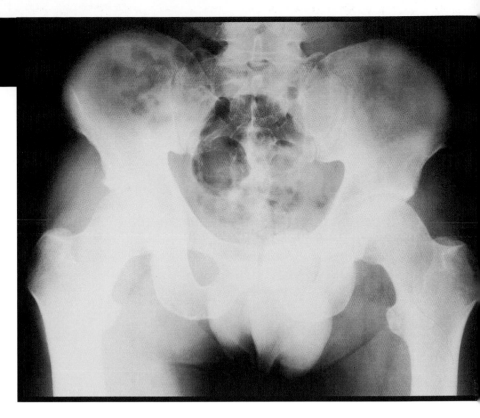

This coloured X-ray shows the male reproductive parts.

upwards into the lower body (abdomen), and then inwards and down, behind the **bladder**. Here it joins the duct from another reproductive part, the seminal vesicle, to form the ejaculatory duct that carries sperm on their journey out of the body.

Seminal vesicles and prostate

The two seminal vesicles, slightly smaller in size and shape than a little finger, lie alongside the end parts of the vas deferens, behind the bladder. They make a fluid that provides sperm cells with **nutrients** and energy. The fluid passes out through a duct at the base of the seminal vesicle, to join the sperm in the vas deferens.

At the point where each ductus deferens joins the seminal vesicle duct, it is called the ejaculatory duct. The two ejaculatory ducts pass through the prostate gland, behind and below the bladder. The prostate is about the size and shape of a chestnut. Like the seminal vesicles, it makes fluids to stimulate and help the sperm on their journey.

Penis

In the base of the prostate, the two ejaculatory ducts join yet another tube, the urethra. When sperm are released, they pass into the urethra, which runs along the inside of the penis, a rod-shaped part in front of the scrotum. The urethra ends as a small opening at the tip of the penis, and this is how sperm leave the male reproductive system.

Two-purpose tube

The tube called the urethra has two main functions. During urination, it conveys the waste liquid urine, which is made by the kidneys, from the bladder out of the body. During **sexual intercourse**, it carries the sperm from the reproductive system, in their fluid, out of the body during ejaculation.

Like an **egg** cell in the female reproductive system, a **sperm** cell in the male reproductive system carries one half of the **genetic** material needed to make a new human being. However, compared to the egg cell, the sperm cell is tiny. It is shaped like a tadpole, with a bulging head, a rod-like middle piece and long, thin, flexible tail. Its total length is 0.05 millimetres, which means 200 sperm cells placed end to end stretch only 1 centimetre. Most of this length is its tail.

Making sperm cells

Like egg cells, sperm cells are made by a special type of cell division, **meiosis**, which halves the genetic material. The female reproductive system works in a cycle of activity, with one egg ripening every 28 days. The male reproductive system works continuously. Sperm cells are being produced all the time, day and night, many thousands each second.

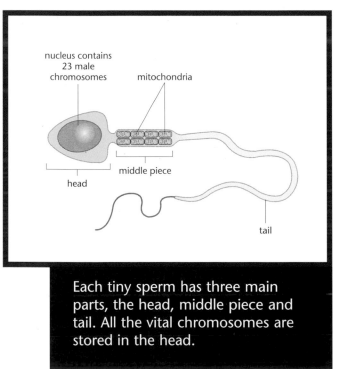

nucleus contains
23 male
chromosomes

mitochondria

middle piece

head

tail

Each tiny sperm has three main parts, the head, middle piece and tail. All the vital chromosomes are stored in the head.

The process of making sperm cells is called spermatogenesis. It takes place in the **testes**, with the final stages in the **epididymes**. Each testis consists of about 800 tiny coiled tubes called seminiferous tubules. Straightened out and joined together, the tubules from one testis would stretch more than 200 metres.

Inside the testis

The inner lining of each tubule contains large rounded cells called spermatogonia. These divide continually to form more cells. As this happens, the cells change shape from rounded to tadpole-like. They also move from the lining around the inner edge of the tubule, towards the space in the middle.

Sperm storage

The resulting spermatids move along their tubules, which join together and carry them into the epididymis. Here they finish their development and become fully mature. The whole process of maturation for a single sperm takes about two months. Each sperm can live for another month, in the epididymis or the first part of the **vas (ductus) deferens**. Sperm that are not released, in the process of ejaculation, break apart and disintegrate, and are replaced by the continuing supply of new sperm cells.

Swimming abilities

Mature sperm lash their long tails to swim towards the female egg cell. However, they need help in their long journey, from the epididymis, along the vas deferens and the urethra, out of the male body during ejaculation, and into the **vagina** of the female, through the **cervix**, into the **uterus**, and then along the **uterine tube**, finally to reach the egg cell. This help is provided by wave-like contractions called **peristalsis** of the muscles in the various tubes and ducts along the route.

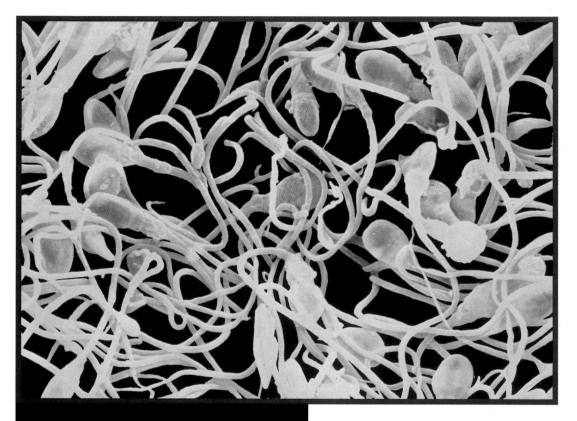

Some 300–500 million active sperm are released during an ejaculation.

Sperm and fluid

The fluid that contains sperm cells is called semen (seminal fluid). It is the combined product from the epididymes, seminal vesicles, prostate gland and other glands. The total volume of the fluid is 3–4 millilitres. Only one-hundredth of its volume is sperm cells – yet there are 300–500 million of them. Too few sperm cells, which is known as a low sperm count, may cause problems in **conceiving** a baby.

Treatment by surgery and/or medical drugs is effective for many problems of the male reproductive system. Treatments vary depending on whether the affected man may want to father children in the future, or not. Also, some problems do not directly affect the workings of the reproductive system, but they can cause pain or irritation that interferes with **sexual intercourse** and so with the ability to have children.

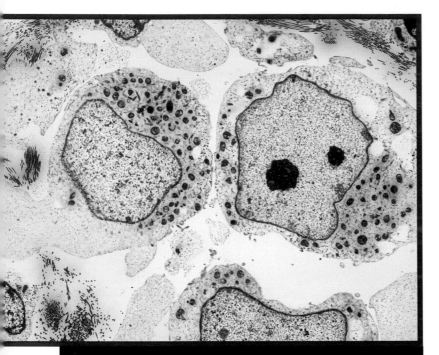

Small samples of cells from the testis, prostate or other male parts are taken by the process called biopsy. They are studied under a microscope, to detect changes such as cancer. These rapidly dividing cancer cells are inside a testis.

Testicular problems

The two **testes** hang loosely in their skin pouch, the **scrotum**. In rare cases, a testis may twist out of position – kinking its **blood vessels**. This is known as testicular torsion and causes pain and swelling. It often occurs for no clear reason. The testis may untwist naturally, but some cases need urgent medical treatment.

Hydrocele is a soft swelling around a testis, caused by an excess of the fluid that normally cushions and protects it within the scrotum. The condition is usually painless or slightly uncomfortable. The fluid can be removed, or its production lessened by a minor operation.

Cysts

Epididymal cysts are bag-like pouches of the **epididymis**, in which sperm and fluid gather. They usually form painless swellings on the upper or side portion of the testis. They may need no treatment unless they become uncomfortable.

Prostate problems

The prostate gland is subject to several conditions. The form of enlarged prostate called benign prostatic hypertrophy, BPH, is non-cancerous. BPH often affects the ability to urinate since the urethra, which carries urine, passes through the prostate and may be narrowed or even squashed closed. Cancer of the prostate can cause similar symptoms. Prostatic cancer is less likely to spread to other body parts, compared to many other forms of cancer. Sometimes it is only discovered at a

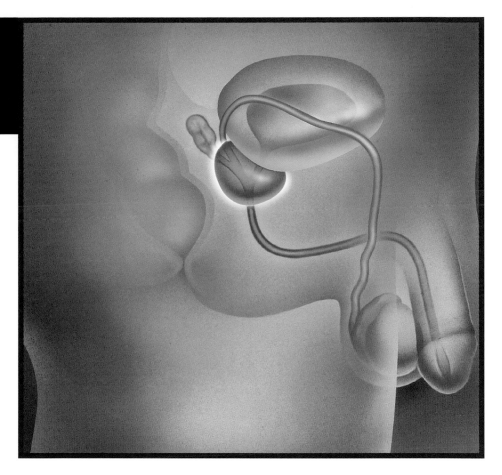

The prostate (blue, upper) wraps around the tubes carrying urine and sperm.

check-up for other health problems and often it progresses slowly. Treatments include various forms of surgery and drugs.

Inguinal hernia

The inguinal canal is a tunnel-like gap through which the testes descend from the **abdomen** into the scrotum below. This usually happens before birth, and the canal is then pressed closed. An inguinal hernia is a weakness in the muscles of the groin area that allows abdominal parts such as the intestine to protrude down the inguinal canal. It shows as a bulge or a dragging feeling in the groin, and needs medical assessment.

Cancer of the testis

Testicular cancer is one of the most common forms of cancer in men, especially between the ages of 20 and 40 years. A growth appears as a lump in the affected testis. The cause is usually unclear. Early detection and treatment has a high success rate, which is one vital reason for regular health checks. In particular, a weekly self-check of the testes is recommended, gently feeling for any changes or unusual swelling, lump, discomfort or pain.

Certain infections by harmful **microbes** (germs) affect the reproductive system directly, as described here. Early treatment by **antibiotic** drugs is very effective in most cases. Some of the infections are sexually transmitted diseases (STD), and venereal diseases (VD) passed on by various forms of sexual contact. Others are not – they spread in other ways. Also some infections, such as HIV/AIDS, may be passed on by sexual contact, but their main effects are elsewhere in the body, not on the reproductive system.

Complications

Reproductive infections may cause inflammation, scarring and blockage of various parts. This can affect general health, the function of the closely connected urinary system, and the ability to have children. Also, a pregnant woman can pass some infections to her baby in the **uterus**, or during birth. In undetected cases the baby is at serious risk of problems such as pneumonia, slow mental development, eye infection or even blindness.

Chlamydial disease

Non-gonococcal urethritis (NGU) or chlamydial disease is due to the **bacterium**-like *Chlamydia trachomatis*. In women it can inflame the urethra, **cervix** and **uterine tubes**, and cause vaginal discharge. In men the urethra, prostate and **epididymes** are usually affected, with discharge from the penis and discomfort or pain. There may be more widespread symptoms such as lung and eye infections.

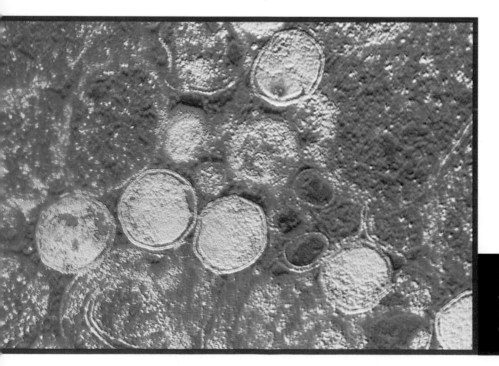

Powerful microscopes are used to look at the microbes that cause Chlamydial disease.

Genital herpes

Also called type II herpes simplex, genital herpes is caused by the *Herpes simplex* **virus** (a type of microbe far smaller than a bacterium). It usually begins with itching and then small, painful blisters on the genital parts. Over a few days these burst and crust over. They may spread, and other symptoms include swelling and pain in the groin, and general fever.

Gonorrhoea

The bacterium *Neisseria gonorrhoeae* can affect the reproductive and urinary systems in both women and men. Symptoms, in both sexes, range from very mild discomfort to urethral and cervical discharge, itching and burning pain and, in men, inflammation of the epididymes in the testicular area. A complication is arthritis or painful joints – gonorrhoea is a leading cause of this problem in young adults.

Syphilis

This dangerous disease, caused by the bacterium *Treponema pallidum*, usually shows as a hard sore or ulcer, called a chancre. This forms where the bacterium entered the body, such as on the genital parts. Further symptoms sometime later include general skin sores and rashes, pains, swollen glands and fever. These may fade, but if not treated, the infection can return with paralysis, mental problems and even death.

Pelvic inflammatory disease

Pelvic inflammatory disease (PID) is a general term for inflammation and infection of the pelvic region – the lower **abdomen** with the reproductive and urinary parts. It is a complication of several reproductive infections. PID can affect the uterus, uterine tubes, **ovaries** and other organs, and the consequences sometimes include the inability to have children.

Reducing risks

The risks of contracting a reproductive system infection, or a general infection that affects other parts of the body, are influenced by several factors. These include the number of different sexual partners, the amount and type of sexual contacts, and personal hygiene measures (see next page). In particular, the spread of HIV/AIDS is greatly affected by sexual factors, and at present, this condition has no cure and is ultimately fatal. Use of a condom can significantly lower the risks.

REPRODUCTIVE HEALTH

Like all body parts, the reproductive system benefits from general health measures. These include a balanced diet, plenty of suitable exercise, sufficient rest and relaxation, and avoiding excess stress and harmful substances, especially certain drugs. There are also many specific measures to maintain reproductive health.

Condoms help to reduce the risk of passing on sexual or genital infections, as well as their use as contraceptives.

Self-awareness

Most doctors recommend regular checks of the reproductive system. Self-examination includes checking for lumps, sore patches, pain, swelling, redness, discharge or other unusual signs. These self-awareness routines include checking the breasts in women, **testes** in men, and the urinary and reproductive openings and general genital area in both sexes.

Vital health checks

There are also 'well person' checks performed by health professionals, including screening services such as the cervical smear test. The frequency of these varies with age, medical and family history, whether a woman has had children, and other factors.

Regular self-examinations and health checks are vital. Some people regard reproductive body parts – even their own – as somehow 'out of bounds' or

Planning children

A woman planning to become pregnant can take various measures to safeguard the health of herself and her baby. In particular, these include stopping smoking (which is always helpful), stopping or minimizing alcoholic drinks, and eating a nutritious, balanced diet. Both tobacco and alcohol, if taken by a pregnant woman, are known to damage the unborn or newborn child.

'different' from other body organs. They may feel awkward or embarrassed about them. However, many problems that affect the reproductive system can be treated much more easily and successfully if they are detected at an early stage.

Hygiene

The external genital parts should be washed and cleaned thoroughly and regularly, as part of normal bodily hygiene. Left unclean, the moist surfaces encourage **microbes** and

A protective guard or box for the genital area is a vital piece of equipment in many sports.

infection. Boys and men should clean under the foreskin (the flap of skin around the front of the penis). A health professional can advise on the correct procedure. Protection from sexually transmitted diseases includes the use of a condom.

Accident and injury

Like any body parts, the genital area and reproductive system are at risk of physical injury or trauma. This occurs especially when there is a blow to the lower **abdomen** or groin, or if the body's weight falls there. The male reproductive parts, being outside the abdomen, are especially at risk.

Apart from pain and damage, even if the injury heals, it can jeopardize the ability to have children in the future. So it is important to wear approved protective clothing and equipment, such as chest-shields for women, athletic supports, jockstraps and box-like guards for men.

The danger of drugs

Drugs such as steroids may be misused in pursuit of building muscles or gaining an advantage in sport. Some of these steroids 'copy' the effects of sex **hormones** such as **testosterone**. They can have very harmful side effects; including damage to the reproductive system that prevents having children in the future.

The central event in normal reproduction is when the **nucleus** (part containing the **genetic** material) of an **egg** cell from the mother joins with the nucleus of a **sperm** cell from the father, to begin the development of a new individual. The joining of the nuclei of the two sex cells, egg and sperm, is known as **fertilization**.

Journey of the egg

The egg or **ovum** is released from the **ovary**, at **ovulation**. Unlike sperm cells, which can 'swim' by lashing their tails, the egg cannot move under its own power. It passes from the ovary into the widened end of the **uterine tube**, and is then carried along towards the **uterus** by two processes. One is **peristalsis** – wave-like contractions of the muscles in the wall of the tube. The other is the flexing of microscopic hairs, called cilia, that line the tube. They swish with a rowing motion like tiny oars.

These two actions create a slow flow of the fluid in the uterine tube, which carries the egg along. Even so, the egg's 10-centimetre journey to the uterus may take between four and seven days.

Journey of the sperm

Sperm cells have a much longer journey than the egg cell. The journey begins in the male's **testes** and **epididymes**, then along the **vas (ductus) deferens**, ejaculatory ducts and the urethra in the penis. The release of many millions of sperm in their fluid, from the male reproductive system, is called ejaculation.

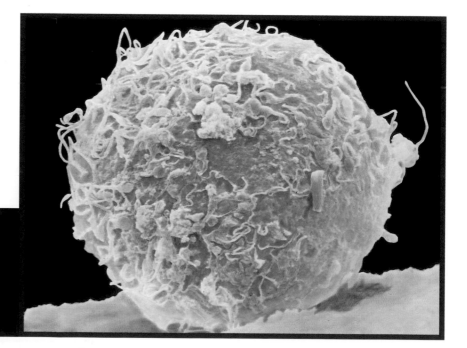

Many sperm gather around the egg, but only one joins with it.

This coloured micrograph shows a single sperm fertilizing a human egg. Of the hundreds of sperm that made it through the uterus to the egg – only this one will succeed in fertilization.

The sperm must negotiate the female **vagina**, **cervix** and **uterus**, where millions become lost or run out of energy. Millions more leave the uterus along the wrong uterine tube, where there is no egg. Even so, many thousands reach the area around the egg cell.

Meeting of egg and sperm

Of the millions of sperm cells, only one can fertilize the egg cell. The sperm's front end, or 'nose cap' comes up against an outer protective layer around the egg cell (zona pellucida). The sperm uses chemicals called **enzymes** to dissolve its way through the protective layer, and the head of the sperm merges with the outer 'skin' or membrane of the egg cell.

The sperm's single, or haploid, set of genetic material (**DNA**), packaged as 23 **chromosomes**, passes into the egg cell. It takes its place alongside the egg's haploid set, also 23 chromosomes of genetic material. This forms the complete or diploid set of genetic material, with 46 chromosomes, so that the fertilized egg can begin development. The outer protective layer of the egg then becomes tougher and harder, to prevent other sperm entering.

Timing of fertilization

The egg cell is viable, or able to be fertilized, for only one or two days after it leaves the ovary. The sperm cells are viable for two to four days (rarely five or six), after their release into the female system. These two time periods must coincide for a sperm to fertilize the egg.

Since an egg cell is usually released on or around day 14 of the **menstrual cycle**, the sperm must arrive a few days before, or after, to make fertilization likely. This 'time window' for fertilization can be used to increase the chances of **conceiving** a child, by knowing when is the best time for conception. It can also be used to avoid conceiving by various natural or calendar methods of contraception.

As the **egg** cell and **sperm** cell join at **fertilization**, the **genetic** make-up of the future human body becomes fixed – including whether it is female or male. There now begins the process of **gestation** or pregnancy, which lasts nine months, until the baby is born.

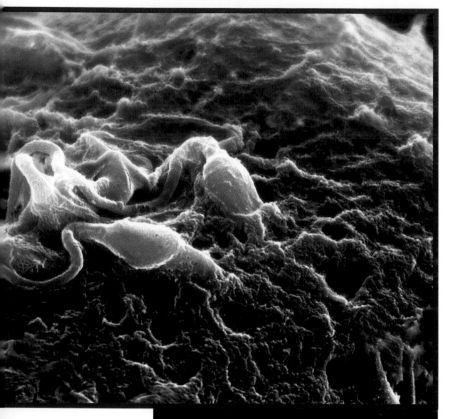

A sperm cell pushes its way through the outer protective layer of the egg cell, so its genetic material can enter the egg.

Early pregnancy

The fertilized egg cell splits into two cells, which each then divide in two, and so on. They increase in numbers by the cell division process of **mitosis**, so that each resulting cell receives the full diploid set of genetic information (**DNA**). The number of cells rises rapidly into hundreds, to form the early **embryo**.

Implantation

A week or so after fertilization the still-microscopic ball of cells implants – it burrows into the soft, blood-rich lining, or **endometrium**, of the **uterus**. This has been prepared by the female cycle to receive and nourish the tiny embryo.

An embryo that implants into another region, such as in the **uterine tube** or even the abdominal cavity, cannot survive. It causes great pain and bleeding and is called an ectopic pregnancy. It is a rare event – each year, only one woman in 15,000 requires treatment for an ectopic pregnancy.

Middle weeks

The cells in the embryo continue to divide, into thousands and millions. About two months after fertilization, the embryo is just 15–20 millimetres long (the size of a small grape). Many of its main body parts and organs are forming. Both male and female embryos are similar at this stage.

The vital stage

From eight weeks after fertilization, the developing baby takes on a recognizable human form and is called a **fetus**. The next two weeks see changes in the internal reproductive parts. In a female fetus, the main reproductive organs become the **ovaries**, while in the male, they become the **testes**. Between weeks 10 and 12 differences become obvious from the outside. The **vagina** forms in a female fetus, and the penis grows in a male one.

Development problems

During these early stages of reproductive system formation, several rare problems may occur and be present at birth. In some cases these malformations are due to inheritance – caused by abnormal genetic material received from one or both parents. In others they are caused by damaging chemicals or conditions experienced by the mother. These include various drugs, harmful rays or radiation (which is why expectant mothers are rarely given X-rays), and infections such as rubella (German measles).

Undescended testes

The male embryo's testes develop inside the **abdomen**. About two months before birth they move, or descend, into the scrotal sac. If they have not descended by birth, this is known as cryptorchism or undescended testes. The descent may still occur naturally, but if delay continues, there is a danger of future fertility problems. Treatment is by an operation or **hormone** tablets.

This ultrasound scan shows an unborn baby, the head at the top right, looking up to the left.

Childbirth is when a baby leaves the **uterus**, passes along the birth canal (**vagina**), and enters the outside world. It usually occurs in three phases.

First stage

The uterus enlarges greatly during pregnancy, and its walls contain some of the body's most powerful muscles. As birth starts the uterus muscles begin to contract, under the influence of the **hormone** oxytocin from the **pituitary gland**. They squeeze the baby against the tightly closed neck of the uterus, the **cervix**.

Gradually the cervix relaxes and widens, or dilates. The mother feels the muscular contractions with great discomfort or pain. They become more powerful and frequent, one every 2 or 3 minutes. The first stage is called labour and lasts, on average, 12–16 hours for the mother's first baby, less for later babies.

At some stage the 'waters break'. The fluid that surrounded and cushioned the baby in the uterus, called amniotic fluid, flows out through the cervix and vagina.

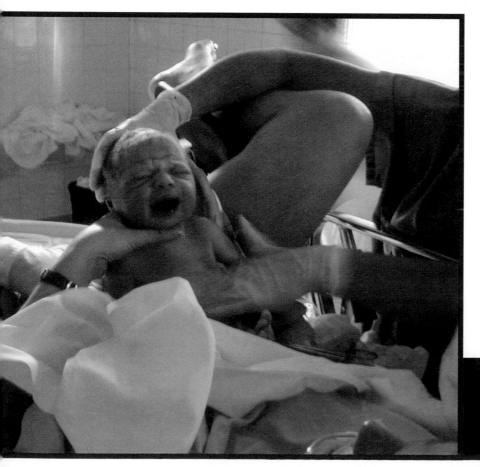

Second stage

Continuing contractions of the uterus muscles push the baby against the cervix, which dilates to about 10 centimetres across. The baby begins to move and passes though the cervix and along the birth canal to the outside. This stage – delivery – may take a couple of hours, or be over in a few minutes.

Birth is strenuous and tiring for both mother and baby, and both need rest afterwards.

Third stage

In the uterus vital **nutrients**, oxygen and other substances pass from mother to baby through the placenta (afterbirth). This disc-shaped part develops in the uterus lining, and is attached to the baby by **blood vessels** known as the umbilical cord. As the baby is born it is still attached to the placenta. In the third stage the placenta frees from the uterus and also emerges. This usually takes 20–30 minutes.

Birth positions

Most babies are born head first. The head is the baby's widest part, and its smooth surface eases the journey through the cervix and birth canal. However the baby may be in a different position, such as buttocks first (breech presentation), or arm or leg first. Attending medical staff may be able to manipulate the baby into the correct position.

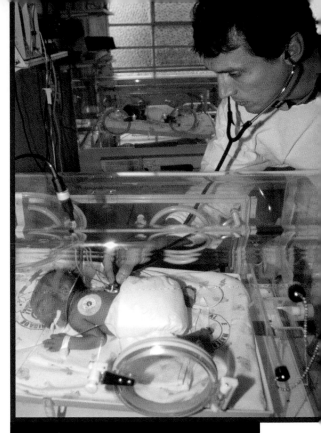

Babies born early, or in poor health, are kept warm and germ-free in an incubator.

Assisted birth

The mother can be given pain relief by breathing in a special gas mixture, or using various types of painkilling drugs. Epidural anaesthesia is the injection of a painkilling drug into the lower back, to block feelings of pain from the lower body.

In case of problems, the birth process can be helped in various ways. Episiotomy is a small incision (cut) to widen the birth canal, so that the baby passes through without the canal tearing. Forceps are curved, paddle-like devices that fit around the baby's head and can change its position or help pull it out. Occasionally a Caesarean section may be needed, for example, if the baby cannot get enough oxygen. The baby emerges via the front of the **abdomen**, through a careful incision made in its wall and the uterus.

Premature birth

In some cases a baby is premature – born before its expected date. Usually, the earlier the birth, the smaller and less developed the baby. Premature babies often need special care. They are kept warm in an incubator, given nutrients and fluid directly into the body, and perhaps given oxygen through a tube into the breathing system. They are also carefully monitored for any signs of illness.

After birth, the baby usually cries to open up its breathing system and take in life-giving oxygen. (In the **uterus** it received oxygen from the mother, in its blood through the placenta and umbilical cord.) Then the baby begins to feed on milk, made in the **mammary glands**, in the breasts.

Hormones and milk

Two reproductive **hormones**, both from the **pituitary gland**, control milk provision. Prolactin stimulates the mammary glands to produce milk. Oxytocin is released in response to touch sensations of the baby suckling. It stimulates the release of milk from the breast, through the nipple. Milk production and release is known as lactation.

For the first day or two, the baby receives not normal milk, but a clearer fluid called colostrum. This is already in the breasts at birth. It is rich in **proteins** and may help to strengthen the baby's **immune system** to resist disease. It also encourages the baby's **digestive system** to begin working regularly. Colostrum is replaced after a couple of days by normal milk.

Weaning

As a baby grows bigger and stronger, the **nutrients** that its body needs change. Gradually mother's milk becomes less suitable and the baby starts to eat 'solids' or normal foods. The time when a baby stops feeding on mother's milk is known as weaning. It is often linked more to social tradition and family lifestyle, than to the baby's nutritional needs.

A small system

The reproductive system is the only main body system that is not working at birth. In fact, it is not yet fully formed. All of its parts are present, but most are relatively small compared to the overall size of the body and its other systems. The reproductive system grows with

Childhood changes

Normally the reproductive organs change little during childhood. Rarely, in a young girl there may be discharge from the **vagina**. This is generally no cause for concern but should be reported to medical staff. In a young boy, the penis may occasionally become stiffer (erection). This is fairly normal, but if it becomes common and frequent, again it should be reported to a doctor. Any signs of redness, swelling, irritation or lumps should receive medical attention.

the rest of the body during childhood, but stays relatively small and non-functioning. There is little obvious outward difference between girls and boys, in terms of overall body size and shape.

From seven or eight years of age, on average, production of reproductive hormones begins to rise slightly. In a girl these are the female sex hormones, **oestrogens**, from the **ovaries**. In a boy they are androgens, chiefly the male sex hormone **testosterone**, from the **testes**. However, the amounts of these hormones are not sufficient to cause any bodily changes, until about ten years of age in girls and twelve years in boys. This marks the early stage of **puberty**.

During childhood, girls and boys are physically similar in overall size and shape, although clothes and hairstyles may differ.

Adolescence is usually described as the stage between childhood and adulthood. It varies hugely between different societies and traditions. In some cases it lasts several years, typically the teenage years, and has its own conventions, customs, fashions and lifestyle. In other cases it occurs over a short time, when a 'rite of passage' event marks the rapid change from girl to woman, or boy to man.

The teenage years may be a time of worries and anxiety, but also an exciting period of rapid physical change and increasing social freedom.

A time of change

Underlying adolescence are changes in the reproductive system. It grows and becomes mature or functioning, able to produce children. This time of bodily change and sexual development is known as **puberty**.

The events of puberty happen at a slightly younger age and closer together over a shorter time, in females compared to males. The average age of puberty in Western societies is about 12 years for females, and 14 for males. The average time taken is 2–3 years for females, and 4 years for boys. However, there is great variation. This is partly due to inherited factors. If a mother went through puberty early, her daughter is likely to, as well.

Worries about puberty

There is considerable variation in the timing of puberty. Some female changes begin at 9 years of age, while some male changes are still occurring at 18. In the great majority of cases, there is no cause for concern. Early or late puberty, including delayed menarche, may cause worry and distress, but a medical check usually provides reassurance.

Female changes

Development of the female body at puberty is due to increasing levels of female **hormones**, **oestrogens**, produced by the **ovaries**. They affect the reproductive system and other body parts:

- the whole body grows much more rapidly, especially in height
- the breasts enlarge, and the nipples become more prominent
- body hair appears, most prominently under the arms and between the legs (pubic hair)
- the main reproductive organs enlarge, and hormonal changes begin the **menstrual cycle**
- the first cycle is known as the **menarche**. It tends to occur when body weight reaches 45–48 kilograms, rather than a certain height or age. In some cases, the first several cycles may not involve actual release of an **egg** cell.
- body proportions change, the hips widen and the body outline becomes more curved.

Male changes

Development of the male body at puberty is due to increasing levels of male hormones, especially **testosterone**, produced by the **testes**:

- the whole body grows much more rapidly, especially in height
- body hair appears, most prominently on the face, under the arms and between the legs (pubic hair)
- the main reproductive organs enlarge, most noticeably the testes in the **scrotum**, and the penis
- the voice 'breaks', or 'cracks' and becomes deeper
- body proportions change, the shoulders broaden and the body outline becomes more angular.

Young males usually begin shaving during puberty, as the amount of facial hair increases.

Varicocele

Varicocele tends to occur in adolescent males. It is due to distended or varicosed veins in the testis. It may cause a swelling around the testis and a dragging ache. Initial treatment is to wear an athletic support. The problem may clear on its own, or with a small operation.

FERTILITY PROBLEMS

Difficulty in **conceiving** a baby is usually called low fertility, while inability to conceive is known as infertility. However the process of reproduction is long and complex and, to some extent, subject to chance. Often, couples who doubted they would ever have a child are suddenly surprised to find they are expecting a new baby.

It takes two

A fertility problem may be based in the male reproductive system, or the female one – or a combination of the two. Inability to conceive is usually regarded first as a feature of both partners, until examinations and tests reveal details.

Lack of 'fertility' may simply be due to lack of understanding about the reproductive process. For example, the **egg** cell can be **fertilized** only during a short part of the **menstrual cycle**, just after egg-release from the **ovary**. So attempts to conceive should be made around this time.

Male problems

A healthy male releases some 300–500 million active **sperm** during ejaculation. It seems to be important that many survive the journey to approach the egg. Together they produce combined amounts of a substance, acrosin, which allows one of them to fertilize the egg. Fewer sperm, known as a low sperm count, may cause reduced fertility – so can sperm that are malformed, or do not swim actively. Sperm are produced continuously by the male reproductive system. However, their numbers may fall due to a problem in the system, such as low **testosterone** production, infection or a growth. Or the cause may be elsewhere in the body, such as general infection or disease, the effects of fatigue, stress or various medications.

Low sperm count is a rare side effect of certain medical drugs and other treatments. Also the production of sperm naturally reduces with age, from 50–60 years, although it can be retained past the age of 75. Problems that interfere with **sexual intercourse** and the release of sperm into the female reproductive system, also affect fertility.

Female problems

Many conditions can affect the balance of **hormones** controlling the menstrual cycle. As in the male, these include conditions elsewhere in the body, such as general infection or disease, the effects of fatigue, stress, severe emotions or certain medications. Problems in the brain or **pituitary gland** also affect fertility, since the pituitary is in overall charge of the hormonal system, including reproductive hormones.

Stress can cause fertility problems for both males and females.

As described earlier, various infections and inflammations can affect the female reproductive system. For example, infection of the **uterine tubes** may cause scarring which blocks the tubes, preventing ripe eggs from passing to the **uterus**.

Various fluids and secretions line the passages of the female reproductive system. In some cases the balance of chemicals can damage the sperm, or the sticky mucus of the cervix lining is too thick for the sperm to get through.

Keeping cool

Sperm are produced most effectively at 35–36 degrees Celsius, slightly lower than normal body temperature. The position of the **testes** in the **scrotum**, below the main body, maintains this cooler temperature. Factors that increase testis temperature, such as fever, or very tight undergarments, can reduce sperm production and affect fertility.

FERTILITY CONTROL

It is not always desirable for **sexual intercourse** to result in a baby. Methods to prevent this are known as fertility control, birth control or contraception. Each method has advantages and disadvantages in effectiveness, ease of use, side effects, convenience and personal preference. For example, the contraceptive pill should be taken at the intervals advised, or it may become much less effective. Also, social customs, traditions and religious beliefs affect the choice of method, or even if one is permitted. Some people choose the single most certain method of contraception, which is to abstain from sexual intercourse.

IU(C)D

The intra-uterine (contraceptive) device is fitted into the **uterus**. It alters conditions slightly so that the **embryo** cannot implant into the uterus lining. There are different shapes and designs of IU(C)D, such as the loop and coil.

Barrier methods

The condom is a flexible rubber bag that fits firmly over the penis. It traps the **sperm** as they are released, so they cannot enter the female system.

The cap and diaphragm are barrier devices that fit firmly over the **cervix**. They prevent sperm from entering the uterus.

Sponges, pads and chemicals

The foam pad or sponge is inserted into the **vagina** and contains spermicide or sperm-killing chemicals. Foams and jellies are available for the same task. They are used just before sexual intercourse, usually combined with other methods.

Uses and risks of the 'pill'

Birth control pills can be used to ease heavy periods and pain and they may protect against ovarian cysts, anaemia, rheumatoid arthritis, breast lumps and certain infections. Some surveys have linked pill use with cancers of the breast and cervix, also high blood pressure, the risk of blood clots (thrombosis) and other problems. However, taken with medical approval and regular checks, most pills are extremely safe.

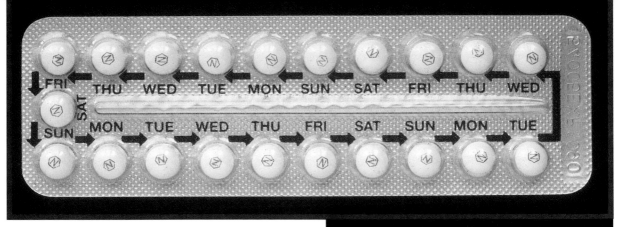

Pills

Birth control pills are also called oral contraceptives. They contain **hormones** that alter the **menstrual cycle**. There are two main types of pill:

- the standard or combined pill contains **oestrogen** and progesterone. They 'trick' the master hormonal gland, the pituitary, into altering the cycle. The result is that the **ovaries** do not release ripe **eggs**, and the lining of the uterus alters so it cannot receive an early embryo.
- the progesterone-only or mini-pill is more suited to women who could be at risk of conditions such as high blood pressure or blood clots.

Contraceptive pills come in a monthly packet. Women who are using the pill, must remember to take one each day.

Timing (calendar or rhythm) methods

Conception can occur only during a few days of the **menstrual cycle**. The calendar or rhythm method is based on avoiding sex during this time. Two techniques make it more accurate. One is measuring the small rise in body temperature (about half a degree) that occurs just after egg release. The other is checking the fluid mucus produced by the cervix, which becomes thinner and clearer a few days before egg release.

Surgical methods

Sterilization is a surgical procedure carried out as a permanent form of birth control:

- in tubal ligation, the **uterine tubes** are tied or cut, so egg cells cannot travel from the ovary to the uterus
- in vasectomy, the **vas (ductus) deferens** tubes are tied or cut, so sperm cannot leave the **testes** and **epididymes**.

These methods are regarded as non-reversible.

How effective?

On average, with sensible use of each method as advised, the different methods of contraception are listed from most to least effective:

- contraceptive pill
- IU(C)D
- condom plus spermicide
- diaphragm plus spermicide
- diaphragm
- timing (calendar or rhythm) methods
- spermicide alone

ASSISTED REPRODUCTION

Recent years have seen great advances in reproductive medicine. Whole new areas of expertise have grown up in the areas of reproduction and **genetics**, based largely on continually improving high-technology procedures and new drugs.

However, the function of the reproductive system is making babies, and babies occupy the emotions, hearts and minds of many people. Birth is also one of the few bodily events subject to laws and regulations. It is not surprising that reproductive medicine generates much discussion.

A slight change in body temperature occurs around ovulation.

'Fertility' drugs

Several **hormone**-containing medications stimulate the ripening and release of **egg** cells. These are used when the **menstrual cycle** is erratic or irregular. However, such medications can have various side effects, including release of several eggs at **ovulation**, which can result in multiple pregnancy.

Surgical methods

Advanced surgical methods can now correct structural problems of the reproductive system, which were almost untreatable several years ago. Micro-surgical equipment and techniques can remove blockages or correct malformations, for example, in the **uterine tubes** or **vas deferens**.

IVF

Normal fertilization takes place in the uterine tube of the female reproductive system. IVF, in vitro fertilization, is when egg and **sperm** are joined outside the body, usually in laboratory equipment. ('In vitro' means 'in glass'. The term 'test-tube baby' is sometimes used, although fertilization is more likely to take place in a flat, round petri dish, than in a test tube.)

Types of IVF

There are many forms of IVF. In the basic method, ripe egg cells are removed from the woman's **ovary** through a small incision (cut) in the **abdomen** and added to sperm cells, in a laboratory container of warm **nutrient** liquid. An egg cell that is fertilized undergoes very early

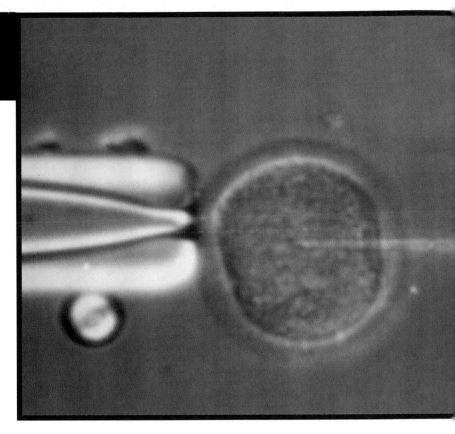

stages of **embryo** formation. It can be identified under a microscope and then inserted into the woman's **uterus**, through the **vagina**, to continue normal development.

Other methods include bringing sperm and egg together in the uterine tube, or replacing the fertilized egg there. The success rate of these procedures is steadily increasing.

Donors and surrogacy

In some cases a man cannot produce sperm cells, or a woman is unable to produce egg cells. Sperm or eggs may then be used from another person – the donor.

In other cases a woman can produce eggs, but she is unable to become pregnant, perhaps because of uterus or hormonal problems. Following IVF, using her egg cell and her partner's sperm, the embryo may be inserted into the uterus of another woman, known as a surrogate mother. The baby is genetically the child of the couple, although it is born to another individual.

Controversies

Advances in reproductive medicine generate much controversy. Background research into assisted reproduction involves 'use' of eggs, sperm and embryos. Should embryos be used and then destroyed in this way? Should a baby have its genetic material changed, by **gene therapy**?

The speed of medical progress has left many people undecided about social and moral issues. This is reflected in official guidelines and regulations, which vary greatly from nation to nation. What is permitted in one country can be illegal in another.

Reproduction relies on **genetics**. The **egg** cell and **sperm** cell each contain a set of human genetic material. These contribute equally to the genetic make-up of the new individual. **Genes** contain the basic instructions for life, development and growth of the human body – including its reproductive system.

Reproduction and chromosomes

As described earlier, human genetic material is in the form of 46 **chromosomes**, containing the substance **DNA**. The chromosomes occur in 23 pairs. One of each pair came from the mother via the egg cell, and one of each pair from the father via the sperm cell.
Of the 23 pairs, 22 are always very similar. In a female the 23rd pair are also very similar in size and shape and both known as X. In a male the 23rd pair differ. One is X. The other is smaller, has a different shape and is known as Y. X and Y are called sex chromosomes.

Male or female?

When sperm or egg cells form in the reproductive system, they contain only one of each pair of chromosomes, including the 23rd pair. So every egg cell contains one X. In the male system, there is an equal chance that either an X or a Y from the 23rd pair will pass into a sperm. So some sperm have an X chromosome, while others have a Y. If an X-carrying sperm fertilizes the egg, the X chromosome will pair with the X in the egg, and the result is XX, a girl. If a Y-carrying sperm fertilizes the egg, the resulting pair will be XY, producing a boy.

IVF has helped many couples to successfully conceive, but it can be a long and stressful process, requiring several treatments and much professional advice.

The male factor

The differences between X and Y chromosomes are very important. Some serious inherited diseases occur only or mainly in males, due to problems on the Y chromosome. These include haemophilia, where the blood does not clot properly to seal a wound.

Advances

In advancing techniques such as IVF, early **embryos** outside the body can be tested to find out whether they are male or female. They can also be tested for the presence of certain genes that may carry inherited conditions. This might allow parents to 'select' which embryo should continue development.

Whatever the scientific advances in the future, reproduction remains the most important and amazing natural process the body has. Without it, there would be no families, and no more people.

Techniques to manipulate the workings of the human reproductive system, genes and the entire reproductive process are progressing rapidly. The future carries hope for some, such as couples wishing to have healthy children, but great worries for others.

Reproduction and life

Reproduction is a central feature of life itself. Yet for an individual person, the parts of the reproductive system are not essential for basic survival. A human body can exist without some, or most of them.

However, for many people, having babies and raising children and being part of a family are central to life's experiences. These activities bring pleasure and joy as well as worry and heartache. It is the 'result' of the reproductive system, when parents have offspring, rather than the system itself, which makes it so important in our lives.

WHAT CAN GO WRONG WITH MY REPRODUCTIVE SYSTEM?

This book has explained the different parts of the reproductive system, why it is essential for life and how it can be damaged by injury and illness. This page summarizes some of the problems that can affect the reproductive system. It also gives you information about how each problem is treated.

Many problems can also be avoided by good health behaviour. This is called prevention. Taking regular exercise and getting plenty of rest are important, as is eating a balanced diet. The table tells you some of the ways you can prevent injury and illness.

Remember, if you think something is wrong with your body, you should always talk to a trained medical professional, like a doctor or a school nurse. Regular medical check-ups are an important part of maintaining a healthy body.

Illness or injury	Cause	Symptoms	Prevention	Treatment
PMS (Pre-menstrual syndrome)	Caused by changing balance of **hormones** and other chemicals in the body a few days before the period starts. Some scientists believe factors like diet and general health can also have an effect.	Changes in mood, feelings and emotions, body changes such as bloated feeling in the stomach.	The causes of PMS are not exactly clear so it is difficult to prevent. Changes in lifestyle, including more exercise, a balanced diet and stopping smoking have been shown to help in some cases.	Doctors may treat PMS by suggesting some lifestyle changes. In severe cases, where PMS interferes with home, school or work life, drugs may be prescribed, including synthetic hormone.
Low **sperm** count	Failure of the **testes** to develop properly, diseases such as mumps, overheating in the scrotal area (the best temperature for sperm production is 33–34°C).	Inability to **conceive** children (no visible sign unless studied under a microscope).	Mumps can be prevented by vaccination, either a single vaccine or the combined MMR (measles, mumps and rubella vaccine).	The effects of low sperm count can be treated by artificial methods of conception and reproduction (see pages 40–41).

Illness or injury	Cause	Symptoms	Prevention	Treatment
Genital herpes	Caused by the *Herpes simplex* **virus**.	Itching and painful blisters in the genital area. Because it is caused by a virus, genital herpes can remain in the body and recur at a later date.	Practising safe sex, using a condom, can lessen the chances of catching most sexually-transmitted diseases.	There is no cure for genital herpes, although antiviral drugs can deal with individual outbreaks.
Cervical cancer	Exact causes are unclear. Cancer is caused by a variety of carcinogenic substances, such as cigarette smoke. It is also thought that some people are naturally more likely to develop cancer than others.	Abnormal **vaginal** discharge and bleeding, pain and general ill health.	We are not yet sure how to prevent cervical cancer but regular cervical smear tests can detect the disease at an early stage when it is much easier to treat. Most deaths from cervical cancer occur in women who have not had these tests.	Treatment may be by a combination of drugs, radiotherapy and surgery to remove the **uterus** and other parts of the reproductive system.
HIV/AIDS	The HIV virus, which can be passed on through body fluids including blood and seminal fluid. The virus can also be passed on to unborn children if their mothers are infected.	After initial symptoms such as fever, sore throats and swollen glands, there are no more symptoms for up to ten years. After this time the body's **immune system** fails because it becomes overloaded and major infections and cancers can develop.	About 90 per cent of people who catch the virus are infected through **sexual intercourse**. Safe sex using a condom will substantially lessen the risks (other methods of contraception such as the contraceptive pill will not protect you against HIV/AIDS). Sharing hypodermic syringes, such as for illegal drug use, is also dangerous.	There is no cure but scientists are working hard to develop a vaccine. Drugs are available that can delay the onset of AIDS but these have serious side effects.

Further reading

The Human Machine, The Production Line: All about your reproduction, Sarah Angliss, Graham Rosewarne (Illustrator) (Belitha Press, 1999)

Human Physiology and Health, David Wright (Heinemann Educational, 2000)

Look at Your Body, Reproduction and Growing Up, Steve Parker (Franklin Watts, 1996)

Need to Know, HIV and AIDS, Sean Connolly (Heinemann Library, 2002)

Need to Know, Sexually Transmitted Diseases, Sean Connolly (Heinemann Library, 2002)

GLOSSARY

abdomen lower part of the main body or torso, between the chest and hips

adolescence time when a child grows rapidly and matures into an adult, physically and mentally, which includes puberty

antibiotic type of medical drug that kills or disables bacteria

bacteria group of micro-organisms that can cause infections

bladder bag-like part of the body in the lower abdomen which stores urine

blood vessels network of tubes that carry blood around the body

cell microscopic unit or 'building block' of a living thing. The body is made of billions of cells.

cervix main opening or 'neck' at the base of the uterus (womb), into the vagina

chromosome thread-like structure in a cell, containing genetic material, DNA

conceive when a new life starts, as sperm joins egg at fertilization

digestive system body parts that take in, break down and absorb foods

DNA deoxyribonucleic acid, the substance that carries genetic instructions (genes)

egg egg cell or ovum, the female reproductive cell

embryo early stage in the development of a living thing – in humans it lasts 8 weeks from fertilization

endometrium inner, blood-rich lining of the uterus

enzyme protein that acts as a catalyst in (speeds up) chemical reactions

epididymis coiled tube next to the testis that stores sperm as they mature

fertilization when an egg cell is joined by a sperm cell and their genetic materials come together

fetus stage in the development of a living thing, after the embryo but before birth

follicle tiny body part like a bag, sac or case – the egg cell ripens in an ovarian follicle

genes instructions for life that exist as genetic material, DNA

gene therapy treatment to cure genetic diseases by introducing normal genes

genetic to do with genes

gestation pregnancy, the time when a baby develops within its mother before birth

hormone natural chemical substance which affects the workings of specific body parts

immune system body's defence mechanisms against infection and disease

ligament strong, slightly stretchy, strap-like part that connects two other body parts

mammary glands female parts specialized to produce milk for the baby

meiosis type of cell division which produces four cells from one, and each resulting cell has half the normal set of genetic material (haploid or monoploid)

menarche time of the first menstrual (female reproductive) cycle

menopause when the female cycle of fertility, the menstrual cycle, ceases

menstrual cycle sequence of events where an egg ripens and the female body becomes ready to nourish an embryo

microbe very small living thing, only visible under a microscope

mitosis type of cell division which produces two cells from one, and each resulting cell has the complete normal set of genetic material (diploid)

nucleus central part of a cell, containing the genetic material

nutrient part of our food that the body can use

oestrogen female hormone that controls the menstrual cycle and sexual development from girl to woman

ovary main female reproductive part which produces ripe eggs and the hormone oestrogen

ovulation release of a ripe egg from the ovary

ovum egg cell or egg, the female reproductive cell

peristalsis wave-like muscle contractions to push or massage substances along

pituitary gland important hormone gland, just below the brain

proteins major group of substances in the body, which form the structural framework of many parts, and also enzymes

puberty sexual development, from child to mature adult

scrotum bag that contains the two main male parts, testes

seminal vesicle small male part that produces fluid to contain sperm cells

sexual intercourse activity involving contact of sexual parts, usually with the penis inserted into the vagina

sperm sperm cell or spermatozoon, the male reproductive cell

testis main male reproductive part which produces sperm and the hormone testosterone

testosterone male hormone that controls sperm production and sexual development from boy to man

uterine tube tube from the ovary to the uterus (also called egg tube or fallopian tube)

uterus womb, a muscular-walled container where a baby develops before birth

vagina part of the birth canal, linking the uterus with the outside

vas (ductus) deferens tube carrying the sperm from the testis and epididymis, on their journey from the body

virus very small micro-organism that can cause infection

INDEX